SUPER EASY

DICTIONARY SKILLS

Paula Pierce

TABLE OF CONTENTS

The dictionary is a book you will use all your life. It provides the reader with a better understanding of words. The dictionary reports six basic facts:

1. How to say the word.

2. How to spell it.

3. The meaning or meanings.

4. The part of speech.

5. Different forms of the word.

6. The history of the word.

Some entries will have illustrations or photographs to help us recognize that particular word.

This workbook explains the basics of the dictionary.

Alphabetizing to the Second Letter

The English language has thousands of words. If listed one after another, finding a single dictionary entry would take a lot of time. Therefore, they are listed in alphabetical (A, B, C) order. All the *A's* are together at the beginning of the book. All the *B's* are next; and so on, to the letter *Z*. Each group is still, really long. Clearly, each word within each letter group, must be alphabetized. So, the 2nd letter of each word is put in order; and the 3rd, and the 4th, and so on, until the words within each letter group are properly placed.

All these words start with the letter *a*:

a d v a n c e

a c o r n

a l l

a a r d v a r k

Look at the second letter of each word. They are different. **Underline the second letter in each word above**. Think about their place in the alphabet by asking:

Which comes first: *d*, *c*, *l*, or *a*?

"*a*" of course!

That is correct; ***aardvark*** would be the first word.

Write the other three words in order below:

1. _____

2. _____

3. _____

Rewrite the words in alphabetical order:

bottle   1. _____

burp   2. _____

baby   3. _____

better   4. _____

Now, try these:

every   5. _____

eon   6. _____

egg   7. _____

Easter   8. _____

How about these?

science   9. _____

since   10. _____

study   11. _____

son   12. _____

Rewrite the words in alphabetical order:

take	1. _____
terrible	2. _____
tidy	3. _____
tuck	4. _____

Set 2

kindergarten	5. _____
keys	6. _____
kabob	7. _____
knife	8. _____

Set 3

upper	9. _____
ugly	10. _____
understand	11. _____
umbrella	12. _____

Rewrite the words in alphabetical order:

hello   1. _____

honey   2. _____

hair   3. _____

high   4. _____

Set 2

sock   5. _____

slice   6. _____

sunny   7. _____

sitting   8. _____

Set 3

enough   9. _____

extra   10. _____

eel   11. _____

egg   12. _____

Rewrite the words in alphabetical order:

gift   1. _____

gate   2. _____

getting   3. _____

great   4. _____

Set 2

box   5. _____

brown   6. _____

burp   7. _____

beak   8. _____

Set 3

fax   9. _____

foot   10. _____

first   11. _____

flock   12. _____

Rewrite the words in alphabetical order:

joke   1. _____

jasmine   2. _____

jumping   3. _____

Jerry   4. _____

Set 2

Celtic   5. _____

chocolate   6. _____

copper   7. _____

close   8. _____

Set3

lamp   9. _____

letters   10. _____

loon   11. _____

lightning   12. _____

Rewrite the words in alphabetical order:

men   1. _____

money   2. _____

many   3. _____

milk   4. _____

Set 2

notes   5. _____

number   6. _____

nest   7. _____

nap   8. _____

Set 3

idle   9. _____

ice cream   10. _____

inner   11. _____

item   12. _____

Rewrite the words in alphabetical order:

dirty   1. _____

dump   2. _____

dry   3. _____

dozen   4. _____

Set 2

bumper   5. _____

basic   6. _____

brown   7. _____

blown   8. _____

----

aspirin   9. _____

ax   10. _____

about   11. _____

atom   12. _____

Rewrite the words in alphabetical order:

everyone   1. _____

elephant   2. _____

extra   3. _____

especially   4. _____

donor   5. _____

dirt   6. _____

date   7. _____

dune   8. _____

obvious   9. _____

oscillate   10. _____

otter   11. _____

oxen   12. _____

Alphabetizing to the Third Letter

Many words in our language have the same second letter. How do we know which is first in the dictionary? Easy! Look at the third letter. All the following words start with the letter **k**:

kept

keep

ketchup

kennel

If you look closer, you will see the second letter is the same, too. **You must look at the third letter to know which word is first in the dictionary.** Look again at the four words. Mark a line through all the **k**'s. Now, mark a line through all the **e**'s. The third letters are:

p, e, t, n

The **e** is the first letter in the alphabet. So, **keep** would be the first word listed in the dictionary. What would be the order of the remaining words?

1. _____

2. _____

3. _____

Rewrite the words in alphabetical order:

medium	1. _____
merge	2. _____
memory	3. _____
measure	4. _____

Set 2

pierce	5. _____
pick	6. _____
pin	7. _____
pipe	8. _____

Set 3

quote	9. _____
quilt	10. _____
queen	11. _____
quarter	12. _____

Rewrite the words in alphabetical order:

harp 1. _____

has 2. _____

hay 3. _____

hat 4. _____

Set 2

burglar 5. _____

bun 6. _____

bugle 7. _____

buck 8. _____

Set 3

Oslo 9. _____

oscillate 10. _____

Osage 11. _____

ostrich 12. _____

Rewrite the words in alphabetical order:

mortgage   1. _____

money   2. _____

mold   3. _____

mock   4. _____

Set 2

rhapsody   5. _____

Rhonda   6. _____

rhyme   7. _____

rhino   8. _____

Set 3

cling   9. _____

club   10. _____

closed   11. _____

clear   12. _____

Rewrite the words in alphabetical order:

tissue 1. _____

title 2. _____

tired 3. _____

tipped 4. _____

Set 2

view 5. _____

vibrant 6. _____

villain 7. _____

vice 8. _____

Set 3

fate 9. _____

fault 10. _____

farm 11. _____

fasten 12. _____

You might wonder… what if all the letters are the same and one word runs out of letters?

> **fiddle**
>
> **fid**
>
> **fiddler**

If the letters are the same until one word runs out of letters, that shorter word will be first in the dictionary. Just being a short word will not place it first! It must have the exact letters until the end of the word. Using this rule, alphabetize the three words above.

1. _____

2. _____

3. _____

Try these:

alphabet   4. _____

alphabetical 5. _____

alpha   6. _____

----

jambalaya 7. _____

jam   8. _____

jamb   9. _____

Rewrite the words in alphabetical order:

rush   1. _____

rust   2. _____

Russia   3. _____

rusk   4. _____

----

redirect   5. _____

redact   6. _____

red   7. _____

redeem   8. _____

----

probably   9. _____

prophet   10. _____

protect   11. _____

prorate   12. _____

----

mole   13. _____

molten   14. _____

mollusk   15. _____

molybdenite   16. _____

Rewrite the words in alphabetical order:

obliterate 1. _____

objective 2. _____

obedient 3. _____

obsolete 4. _____

----

platoon 5. _____

plus 6. _____

plesiosaur 7. _____

plight 8. _____

----

cyclone 9. _____

cygnet 10. _____

Cypress 11. _____

cynical 12. _____

Entry Words

The words listed in a dictionary are called *entry words* and will be set in **dark, bold print**:

> **de cath lon,** (di kath´lon), *n.* a ten part contest in which athletes compete against each other.

> **de cay,** (di kā), *v.t.* 1. to rot, decompose. 2. to lose strength or power.

The above entry words are listed in a much **bolder** print than the information about the words. Open any page in your dictionary and list two **entry words**. On what page were they listed?

Page _____

1. _____

2. _____

How did you know they were entry words?

3. _____

Turn to page 37 in your dictionary. Copy 3 consecutive[1] entry words below:

4. _____

5. _____

6. _____

[1] **Use your dictionary to discover the meaning of this word.**

eye sight, (ī sīt), *n.* 1. able to see. 2. how far one can see.

eye sore, (ī sor), *n.* an unpleasant sight.

Write the above entry words:

1. _____

2. _____

----

jel ly roll, (jel′ ē rōl), *n.* a thin layer of cake with a center of jelly.

Je na, (yā nä), *n.* an East German city.

Write the above entry words:

3. _____

4. _____

Turn to page 65 in your dictionary, Copy 3 consecutive entry words:

5. _____

6. _____

7. _____

perpendicular 1. _____

pet 2. _____

patent 3. _____

Perseus 4. _____

Rugby 5. _____

rubbed 6. _____

rugged 7. _____

ruff 8. _____

----

curious 9. _____

curd 10. _____

curb 11. _____

cure 12. _____

----

apparel 13. _____

apostrophe 14. _____

ant 15. _____

answer 16. _____

fauna, (fô´ nə), **_n._** the animal life of a particular region.

follow, (fol´ ō), **_v.t._** to come after.

free, (frē), **_adj._** liberty; not controlled by another.

Write the above dictionary entry words:

1. _____

2. _____

3. _____

Rewrite the words in alphabetical order:

gyp   4._____

gurgle   5 _____

good   6. _____

grave   7. _____

----

patsy   8. _____

polish   9. _____

petrol   10. _____

pet   11. _____

Guide Words

Let's review:

1. All entries in the dictionary are in alphabetical order.

2. If looking for a word that begins with the letter *r*, it is not hard to find the *r*'s in the dictionary.

3. Even though many words begin with the letter *r*, they are easily located by looking at the 2nd, 3rd, etc. letters in the words.

But that is still a lot of looking! So, very special words were placed in the dictionary to help. At the **top** of every page are **two** words. The word on the top **left side** of the page is the **first entry word** on that page. *However, it is not necessarily the very first word on that page.* Sometimes, the definition of the last word (on the page before) must continue to the next page. The word on top **right side** of the page will be the **last entry word** on that page. Likewise, it may not be the actual last written word on that page. If the word you are looking for comes after the left guide word but before the right guide word, it will be on that page. It is simply a matter of putting your word between those two guide words. If it fits in the middle of the two guide words alphabetically, it will be on that page.

Let's say you need to find the word *beat* in the dictionary. Just check the guide words at the top of the page to see if *beat* will fit between them. It is just like alphabetizing the three words.

muzzle like that of a dog.

ba by, (bā´ bē), *n.* 1. An infant. 2. someone who acts like a young child.

bab ble, (bab´ l), *v.* speech that is not understood.

back, (bak), *n.* the opposite part of the body from the front.

bad, (bad), *adv.* wicked, evil.

bag, (bag), *n.* a container. usually cloth or paper, which holds other things.

bal let, (ba´ lā), *n,* a graceful form of dancing.

beak, (bēk), *n.* the bill of a bird.

bear, (´ber), *n.* a large animal with thick fur.

beat, (bēt), *v.* to hit, whip or strike something.

bed, (bed), *n.* 1. something to sleep on. 2. a base on which an object might rest. 3. ground under the river.

big, (big), *adj.* 1. not small. 2. grown up. 3. a great event.

bill, (bil), *n.* 1. money owed. 2. paper money. 3. bird's beak.

bind, (bīnd), *v.* to tie together.

black, (blak), *adj.* the color of coal or tar.

The word *beat* is on this page because it fits alphabetically between the two entry words.

left guide word: **baby**

beat

right guide word: **black**

Use the dictionary excerpt on page 25 to answer the following questions:

1. What is the guide word on the left top side of the page?

_____

2. Is it the same word as the first **entry** word (hint: not necessarily the actual first word on the page)? _____

3. What is the guide word on the right side of the page?

_____

4. Is it the same word as the last **entry** word on the page (hint: not necessarily the last actual word on the page)? _____

When using guide words, it is never harder than putting three words in alphabetical order. That is what you are doing! For example, when trying to locate the word:

pickle

It must fit between the two guide words, just as it would if you were alphabetizing it. Simply see if it fits in the middle!

left guide word   right guide word

picker   **picotee**

picker

pickle

picotee

It definitely fits between the two guide words. **It is on that page**.

Put an **X** in front of the entry words that would fit between these guide words. You may use a separate sheet of paper to alphabetize them.

exterior   **face**

_____ fog

_____ fortune

_____ extraneous

_____ expel

abundant   **act**

_____ above

_____ action

_____ accident

_____ abdomen

hollow   **horoscope**

_____ hot

_____ Holland

_____ hopeful

_____ hut

Open a dictionary to page 54. Write the guide words on that page.

1. left guide word _____

2. right guide word _____

Write the first three **entry** words on page 54 (hint: not necessarily the actual first three words).

3. _____

4. _____

5. _____

Write a word that would not fit on page 54.

6. _____

Would the word you chose fit between the guide words on

page 54? 7. _____

Rewrite the words in alphabetical order:

something   1. _____

slept   2. _____

should   3. _____

stairs   4. _____

----

people   5. _____

plump   6. _____

python   7. _____

physical   8. _____

----

likely   9. _____

lovely   10. _____

leak   11. _____

lucky   12. _____

Rewrite the words in alphabetical order:

tomato	1. _____
toxin	2. _____
today	3. _____
toast	4. _____

floor	5. _____
flat	6. _____
flute	7. _____
flesh	8. _____

mighty	9. _____
minute	10. _____
midway	11. _____
mite	12. _____

Parentheses

Let's review:

1. Dictionary entry words are listed in **bold print**.

2. All entry words are listed in alphabetical order.

3. Guide words show the first and last entry words on each page.

( ) These are called **parentheses**.

They are used to add extra information. In the dictionary, parentheses help you read a word more easily. This is important since our 26 letters make 40 different sounds! Quite often, words are not spelled the way they sound. In most dictionaries, entry words are listed; followed by a spelling that shows the way they would sound if they didn't have:

extra letters

silent letters

special blended letters

& all those other weird things our language does!

These helpful spellings are surrounded by parentheses and listed right after the entry words:

ba by, (ba´ be)

It is easy to find the way a word is pronounced by looking:

INSIDE THE PARENTHESES.

For example, the word back would be presented as:

back, (bak)

The entry word **back** is written with a **ck,** but only the **k** is heard when pronounced. So, inside the parentheses, only the **k** is written.

note, (nōt)

1. Is the word **note** pronounced with a long or short **o**? _____

2. What sound does the e on the end of the word make?

_____

Open a dictionary to page 77. Write the first three entry words. Next, write the spellings in the parentheses.

_____, ( )

_____, ( )

_____, ( )

Reading Dictionary Markings

Say these vowels: ā ē ī ō

If you look inside the parentheses, you can tell the sounds vowels make by the marks above them. Look at the line above each vowel. It is called a **macron**, and informs you that the vowel will say its name.

Say these words:

ōats   met   pīne   cāke

1. What word above does not contain a long vowel? _____

2. What word below does not contain a long vowel? _____

sō   ēve   ācorn   sit

3. Put a macron (line) over the vowels that make a long sound:

he   time   help   hose

4. What does the line over a vowel tell us?

      a) It makes a short sound.

      b) It makes a long sound.

5. What is the name of the line over a vowel? (hint: it tells you on

   this page. _____

What about the **u**? It isn't marked with the macron because when you say **u**; you are actually saying **yü**. To further complicate the situation, it is not marked the same way in every dictionary. Some dictionaries will mark it with a **ū**; but more often, it will be marked **yü** or **yoo**. Just be aware; the **u** is special.

use, (yüz, yooz, üz, or ūz)

U-boat, (yü´ bōt, ü´ bōt, or ū bōt)

Remember, *diacritical marks* (name given to pronunciation markings in a dictionary) vary depending on the dictionary. The pronunciation key (in the front of the dictionary) will help you understand what markings are used.

Put a macron over each underlined vowel if it says the long vowel sound. Circle the underlined vowels that are not long.

1. b <u>a</u> b y   2. <u>a</u> p p l e   3. t o d <u>a</u> y

4. r <u>i</u> g   5. <u>o</u> p e n   6. <u>e</u> n o u g h

Set 2

7. g <u>a</u> m e   8. d <u>o</u> l l   9. t <u>a</u> k e

10. s <u>a</u> y   11. b <u>e</u> t   12. b <u>a</u> t

Macrons are marks put over vowels that make a long sound; however, the **short** vowels have **no markings!**

13. How are long vowels marked in the dictionary?

_____

14. How are short vowels marked in the dictionary?

_____

Say these dictionary entry words (hint: pronunciation help is in the parentheses):

press,   (pres)

dive,   (dīv)

beak,   (bēk)

seal,   (sēl)

Sometimes, a word sounds just like it is spelled:

punt,   (punt)

had,   (had)

plug,   (plug)

Sometimes, words have more than one syllable (sound):

1.____   **library,**   (lī bre rē)

2.____   **cunning,**   (kun ing)

3.____   **reply,**   (rē plī)

4. ____   **nibble,**   (nib l)

Do you see that each syllable is separated?

Write the number of syllables in front of each word.

1. Circle the word that has the same **e** sound as in the word **bed**, (bed).

   (Hint: Look inside the parentheses at the **e** in bed. The correct word will

   have an **e** that is marked exactly the same).

   deserve,   (di zurv)

   exit,   (eg zit)

   recital,   (ri sīt l)

2. Circle the word that has the same **o** sound as in the word **flock,** (flok):

   goal,   (gōl)

   throat,   (thrōt)

   wasp   (wosp)

3. Circle the word that has the same **a** sound as in the word **made,** (made):

   laden,   (lād n)

   medal,   (med l)

   amble,   (am bl)

4. Circle the word that has the same **u** sound as in the word **hug** (hug):

   use,   (yüz)

   love,   (luv)

   fuse,   (fyüz)

1. Circle the word with the same **a** sound as in the word

comrade, (kom r**a**d).

> **pain,** (p ā n)
>
> **masthead,** (m a s t h e d)
>
> **palooka,** (p ə l ü k ə)

It doesn't matter for now, if you do not recognize the other strange markings. They will be discussed later. Just look for the same diacritical mark as in the example word.

----

2. Circle the word with the same <u>short</u> **u** sound as in the word

rusticate, (r**u**s tə kāt).

> **Duma,** (d ü m ə)
>
> **guardian,** (g ä r d ē ə n)
>
> **mumble,** (m u m b ə l)

----

3. Circle the word with the same **a** sound as in the word

plague, (pl**ā**g).

> **republican** (r i p u b l ə k ə n)
>
> **scarecrow** (s k e r k r ō)
>
> **bagel** (b ā g ə l)

$$\bar{a} \qquad \bar{e} \qquad \bar{i} \qquad \bar{o}$$

1. How do you know these are long vowels?

_____

2. Write the above vowels and show them long.

_____

3. Write the above vowels and show them short.

_____

4. What is the difference?

_____

5. To find out how to say a new word we look inside the:

_____.

6. You can tell how many syllables a word has because they are:

_____.

The Schwa

Sometimes vowels make sounds that are not exactly long or short! If a vowel has an **a** sound as in the word **ago**, the **a** sound is neither long, nor short. It sounds more like the noise someone might make if they were hit in the belly-- **uh**. A special diacritical mark is used in the dictionary to show this sound: ə. Looks like an upside down **e**; doesn't it? Do you remember this mark from page 38? This symbol for the **uh** sound is called a **schwa**. When this marking is used, you know to say the hit-in-the-belly sound! Remember, ə = **uh**.

Here are some examples:

item	(ī təm)
atom	(a təm)
pencil	(pen səl)

Say these words:

chuckle	(chuk əl)
oven	(uv ən)
lodger	(lo jər)
affliction	(ə flik shən)

Which word has the same e sound as in the word pattern, (pat ərn)?

engage	(in gāg)
reading	(rēd ing)
maple	mā pəl)

Stressed and Unstressed Syllables

Did you wonder why the short, unmarked **u** isn't used instead of the schwa? After all, the schwa does sound like a short **u**. The answer involves words with more than one syllable.

In a multi-syllable word, one syllable has more "sound power" than the other syllables. The syllable with the most sound is called the **stressed** syllable. The syllables that do not sound as much are called the **unstressed** syllables.

The schwa (uh sound) **is never found in the most stressed syllable.** Can you hear the schwa sound in these words?

a bout	(**uh** bout)	or	(ə bowt)
tak en	(tāk **uh**n)	or	(tāk ən)
pen cil	(pen s**uh**l)	or	(pen səl)
lem on	(lem **uh**n)	or	(lem ən)

The part of the word that sounds the most is <u>not</u> the schwa syllable. These were easy words we already know how to pronounce. However, when we see an unknown word, being able to stress each syllable correctly will help us say the word properly. Many times, people from other countries learn English but do not stress the syllables correctly. The words sound a little strange to us.

An accent mark is placed by the syllable with the most stress. This is another time when dictionaries differ. The accent mark will be placed *before*, *after*, or *over* a stressed syllable. We will use the accent mark **after** the stressed syllable in this workbook since it is the most commonly used in student dictionaries. When this mark: ´ is at the end of a syllable, remember it is the most stressed.

Let's look at those words again:

a bout	(ə bowt´)
tak en	(tāk´ ən)
pen cil	(pen´ səl)
lem on	(lem´ ən)

Think about how different these words would sound if the schwa syllables were stressed! Try it. Sounds weird, doesn't it?

Turn to the dictionary excerpt on page 25. Find the three words with stress marks. Write them below.

1. _____

2. _____

3. _____

Put stress marks on each word (remember the rule for the schwa):

1. **pocket,**   (pok   ət)

2. **nibble,**   (nib   əl)

3. **blubber,**   (blub   ər)

4. **chicken,**   (chik   ən)

5. **shiver,**   (shiv   ər)

6. **writer,**   (rīt   ər)

7. **temper,**   (tem   pər)

8. **policeman,**   (pə   lēs   mən)

Two different **u** sounds are in the word nuzzle:

nuzzle, (nuz′ əl)

It makes sense that the short **u** is the stressed syllable because the other syllable contains a schwa. The schwa syllable is never stressed. Read the following sentence aloud:

The schwa is not used in stressed syllables

Write the number of syllables in each word.

Circle the stressed syllable.

1. ____ **performance**   (pər for′ məns)

2. ____ **outfielder**   (owt′ fēld ər)

3. ____ **language**   (lan′ gwij)

4. ____ **especially**   (ə spesh′ əl ē)

5. ____ **mandolin**   (man′ dl in)

6. ____ **engineer**   (in jə nēr′)

7. ____ **credibility**   (kred′ ə bil ə tē)

8. ____ **inhalation**   (in hə lā′ shən)

9. ____ **plateau**   (plat ō′)

10. ____ **twenty**   (twen′ tē)

Primary and Medium Accent Marks

We have learned that ´ is a stress mark and it tells which syllable has the most sound. Study the entry word below:

mathematical   (math´ ə mat´ ə kəl)

There are two stress marks! One is darker than the other. This is necessary because in words with many syllables, there is a **primary stress** (the syllable with the most stress) and a **medium stress** (stressed but not as forceful as the primary stress syllable). Say the word. These two syllables are stressed more than the others; however, you do hear the primary syllable as the most forceful.

Since the medium stress mark is only in words with three or more syllables, it will not be used as often. In fact, some dictionaries only mark the primary syllable. Also, markings vary according to the dictionary used. Just remember, the schwa will not be a primary accented syllable.

The Umlaut ä

In the word **father**, the **a** sounds like a short **o**. In the dictionary, the diacritical mark for this vowel sound is an **a** with two dots over it. This mark is called an **umlaut** (oom lowt) An umlaut is used for vowels with special pronunciations. Say these words using the umlaut for the **a** with a short **o** sound.

amen   (ä men)

ankh   (ängk)

garage   (gə räzh)

what   (hwät)

want   (wänt)

Unfortunately, different dictionaries have different markings! To keep from getting confused, always check the pronunciation key in your dictionary. The key displays the symbols the way they chose to present them. Here is an example of an entry word from two different dictionaries.

what   (hwät)

what   (hwot)

If you do not recognize all of the diacritical marks in your dictionary, check the pronunciation key. Study the symbols used for the letter **a** in one dictionary:

a as in **hat, cap**

ā as in **age, face**

ä as in **father, far**

This dictionary gives two word examples for each of the vowel's diacritical marks. When you see an unmarked **a** in this particular dictionary, the vowel will make a short sound like in the words: **hat** & **cap**. This lets you know to say the short **a** sound to all unmarked **a**'s. Likewise, every **a** with a macron will have a long vowel sound.

ā age, face

Suppose you look up the word: microtubule. The entry word will probably look like this:

microtubule   (mī krō tü´ byül)

Perhaps you don't know what the **ü** means. Go to the pronunciation key and look for that symbol:

u as in cup, butter

ü as in rule, move

It becomes much easier to say the word when you know the **ü** sounds like: rule & move.

Now try the word: **mī krō tü´ byül**.

Study this pronunciation key:

a = rat	**o** = rot	**i** = it
ā = age	**ō** = over	**ī** = ice
ä = tar	**ô** = cord	**u** = cup
e = bet	**oi** = oil	**ü** = rule
ē = beat		

ə = **a** as in **a**bove
e   **o**ven
i   p**e**ncil
o   auth**o**r
u   medi**u**m

The above key helps to decode these words:

hallucination   (hə lü´ sn ā shən)

nitrogen   (nī´ trō jən)

clannish   (klan´ ish)

smeary   (smir´ ē)

Teutonic   (tü ton´ ik)

fiancé   (fē än sā´)

cordon bleu   (kôrd´ on blü)

admittedly   (ad mit´ id le)

Remember to check the pronunciation key because different dictionaries have different markings!

Use the dictionary excerpt to answer the questions:

kame, (kām), *n.* an icy hill of a glacier.

kapok, (kā′ pok), *n.* fibers of a silky cotton tree used for stuffing pillows.

languor, (lan′ gər), *n.* lack of vigor; weakness.

lignite, (lig′ nīt), *n.* coal created from decomposed vegetables.

mispronounce, (mis′ prō nouns′), *v.t.* to say a word wrong.

---

1. A sickness might cause:

   a) kapok

   b) languor

   c) kame

2. How many syllables are in the word **mispronounce**?

   a) one

   b) two

   c) three

3. From the above entry words, which word is spelled correctly?

   a) langer

   b) lignite

   c) came

Using the Dictionary

Study the dictionary excerpt:

baby	**black**

ba by, (bā′ bē), *n*. 1. an infant. 2. someone who acts like a young child.

bab ble, (bab′ l), *v*. speech that is not understood.

back, (bak), *n*. the opposite part of the body from the front.

bad, (bad), *adj*. not good.

bag, (bag), *n*. a container usually cloth or paper, which holds other things.

bal let, (ba′ lā) (ba lā′), *n*. a graceful form of dancing.

beak, (bēk), n. the bill of a bird.

bear, (ber), *n*. a large animal with thick fur.

beat, (bēt), *v*. to hit, whip or strike something.

bed, (bed), *n*. 1. something to sleep on. 2. a base on which an object might rest. 3. ground under a river.

big, (big), *adj*. 1. not small. 2. grown up. 3. a great event.

bill, (bil), *n*. 1. money owed. 2. paper money. 3. bird's beak.

bind, (bīnd), *v*. to tie together.

black, (blak), *adj*. the color of coal or tar.

1. The darkened words are entry words.

2. The spelling in the parentheses tells the way it is pronounced & stressed.

3. The darkened letter or abbreviation tells the word's part of speech.

The abbreviated letters represent:

n. = noun	***prep.*** = preposition
v. = verb	***pro.*** = pronoun
vt. = verb transitive	***conj.*** = conjunction
adj. = adjective	***adv.*** = adverb

This is standard for most dictionaries; however, check the pronunciation key!

Write each word's part of speech using the dictionary excerpt (p.50).

1. babble _____

2. baby _____

3. big _____

4. bind _____

5. beat _____

Open your dictionary to the first entry word in the **A**'s. Write the word and its part of speech.

6. _____ 7. _____

Open your dictionary to the last entry word in the **Z**'s. Write the word and its part of speech.

8. _____ 9. _____

Word Meaning

The most common reason for using the dictionary is to find a word's definition. In the English language that can be complicated. Many of our words have several meanings. For example:

fly, (flī), *n*. 1. an insect that has one set of transparent wings; housefly. 2. fishhook. 3. a thing that ruins something, *fly in the ointment*. 4. the zipper flap on pants. 5. space above the stage door. 6. the flap forming the door of a tent.

fly, (flī), *v*. 1. to move through the air with wings or an airplane. 2. to pilot a plane. 3. lose control of emotions, *fly off the handle*. 4. object being carried through the air, *let it fly*.

Look at all those meanings! It is hard to believe one little three-letter-word could mean so much. You can see why a dictionary is a very important tool!

Fortunately, all our words do not have so many meanings. It sure is nice to have a book that tells so many things about our words.

Study the entry words below:

im mor tal, (im ôr´ tl), *adj*. living forever; never die.

in ar tic u late, (in är tik´ yə lit), *adj*. not able to speak in words.

lat i tude, (lat´ ə tüd), *n*. distance north & south measured in degrees [about 69 miles each].

ma tri arch, (mā trē ärk), *n*. mother who is the leader of the family or tribe.

1. What sentence uses the word **immortal** correctly?

   a) He ate a small immortal of cookie.

   b) The wind immortals very hard in the winter.

   c) The superhero was immortal.

   d) He sailed 69° immortal.

2. What sentence uses the word **matriarch** correctly?

   a) The soldiers matriarch the battlefield.

   b) The matriarch took good care of her family.

   c) The egg was matriarch shaped.

3. What sentence uses **inarticulate** correctly?

   a) Cows and pigs are inarticulate.

   b) The pilot inarticulate the plane.

   c) The inarticulate was built last year.

   d) She spent all of her inarticulate.

English Word History

Our language started long ago on a small island called Britannia (now Great Britain). The poor uneducated farmer/hunters were continually conquered by warring armies. When a new military force took over, it brought a new language with it. Foreign words were heard and included in the Brit's vocabulary resulting in a language known as *Old English* (450 A.D. to 1150 A.D.). It wasn't the English we know today! With each military defeat, new words were introduced. The French began to influence our language when William the Conqueror of France invaded in 1066 A.D. William and his people were far more sophisticated than the poor, defeated Brits. Remember, these poor island people had **no education**; which was the <u>main cause</u> for their constant defeat. New, refined words were introduced, and over time, more than one word was used for the same thing. This is one reason our language is so difficult to learn. We don't just say we're *sad* but miserable, unhappy, cheerless, sorrowful, forlorn, or down. The language changed slowly until it melted into *Middle English* (1150A.D. to 1500 A.D.). During this time period, the printing press was invented creating an accepted way to spell English words. In addition, trading goods with other nations and the writings of poets brought our language to Modern English (1500 A.D. to Present). But it isn't over yet! New words due to inventions and technology are still being created; as well as, new ways to express ourselves.

Some dictionaries include the origin of a word. It may say OE (Old English) or L (Latin). Check the key to see what the abbreviations mean.

Dictionary Skills Final Test

1. Circle the entry word that would use these guide words:

lightning   **little**

lethargic

line

look

----

2.   **polish**   **prefer**

policy

prevail

popcorn

Write the number of syllables in each word:

3. _____ astounding   (ə stound′ ing)

4. _____ comfortable   (kum′ fər tə bəl)

5. _____ nationalism   (nash′ ə nə liz′ əm)

4. What word contains both primary and medium stress marks?

Rewrite the words in alphabetical order:

impeach   6. _____

idea   7. _____

iceberg   8. _____

impede   9. _____

Rewrite the words in alphabetical order:

land   10. _____

lamp   11. _____

lament   12. _____

lame   13. _____

----

for tis si mo, (fôr tis´ sē mō), *adj.*, adv. in music, very loud.

nat ur al, (nach´ ər əl), *adj.* not made by man; created by nature.

o rang u tan, (ô rang´ ü tan), *n.* a large ape with long arms & reddish hair.

Use the dictionary excerpt to answer the questions.

14. Fill in the word that correctly completes this sentence:

    The huge _____ scared the children.

15. Fortissimo has _____ syllables.

16. What sentence uses the word **natural** correctly?

    ○ The new overpass bridge was a beautiful <u>natural</u> structure.

    ○ Yellow Stone Park has many <u>natural</u> wonders.

    ○They went to the <u>natural </u> for lunch every day at noon.

17. What word is used when speaking of music?_____

Answer Key

4.

1. baby	5. Easter	9. science
2. better	6. egg	10. since
3. bottle	7. eon	11. son
4. burp	8. every	12. study

5.

1. take	5. kabob	9. ugly
2. terrible	6. keys	10. umbrella
3. tidy	7. kindergarten	11. understand
4. tuck	8. knife	12. upper

6.

1. hair	5. sitting	9. eel
2. hello	6. slice	10. egg
3. high	7. sock	11. enough
4. honey	8. sunny	12. extra

7.

1. gate	5. beak	9. fax
2. getting	6. box	10. first
3. gift	7. brown	11. flock
4. great	8. burp	12. foot

Answer Key (pages 8-12)

Page:

8.

1. jasmine	5. Celtic	9. lamp
2. Jerry	6. chocolate	10. letters
3. joke	7. close	11. lightning
4. jumping	8. copper	12. loon

9.

1. many	5. nap	9. ice cream
2. men	6. nest	10. idle
3. milk	7. notes	11. inner
4. money	8. number	12. item

10.

1. dirty	5. basic	9. about
2. dozen	6. blown	10. aspirin
3. dry	7. brown	11. atom
4. dump	8. bumper	12. ax

11.

1. elephant	5. date	9. obvious
2. especially	6. dirt	10. oscillate
3. everyone	7. donor	11. otter
4. extra	8. dune	12. oxen

12.

1. kennel

2. kept

3. ketchup

Answer Key (pages 13-17)

Page:

13.

1. measure	5. pick	9. quarter
2. medium	6. pierce	10. queen
3. memory	7. pin	11. quilt
4. merge	8. pipe	12. quote

14.

1. harp	5. buck	9. Osage
2. has	6. bugle	10. oscillate
3. hat	7. burglar	11. Oslo
4. hay	8. bun	12. ostrich

15.

1. mock	5. rhapsody	9. clear
2. mold	6. rhino	10. cling
3. money	7. Rhonda	11. closed
4. mortgage	8. rhyme	12. club

16.

1. tippet	5. vibrant	9. farm
2. tired	6. vice	10. fasten
3. tissue	7. view	11. fate
4. title	8. villain	12. fault

17.

1. fid	4. alpha	7. jam
2. fiddle	5. alphabet	8. jamb
3. fiddler	6. alphabetical	9. jambalaya

Answer Key (pages 18-23)

Page:

18.
1. rush	5. red	9. probably	13. mole
2. rusk	6. redact	10. prophet	14. mollusk
3. Russia	7. redeem	11. prorate	15. molten
4. rust	8. redirect	12. protect	16. molybdenite

19.
1. obedient	5. platoon	9. cyclone
2. objective	6. plesiosaur	10. cygnet
3. obliterate	7. plight	11. cynical
4. obsolete	8. plus	12. Cyress

---

20   Page numbers will vary. Answers vary.

21.
1.eyesight	3. jelly roll	5-7 Answers vary.
2. eyesore	4. Jena	

22.
1. patent	5. rubbed	9. curb	13. answer
2. perpendicular	6. ruff	10. curd	14. ant
3. Perseus	7. Rugby	11. cure	15. apostrophe
4. pet	8. rugged	12. curious	16. apparel

23.
1. fauna	4. good	8. patsy
2. follow	5. grave	9. pet
3. free	6. gurgle	10. petrol
	7. gyp	11. polish

Answer Key (pages 26-32)

Page:

26.   1. baby   2. yes   3. black   4. yes

---

27.   1. extraneous

            2. accident

            3. hopeful

---

28.   Answers vary.

---

29.   1. should   5. people   9. leak

            2. slept   6. physical   10. likely

            3. something   7. plump   11. lovely

            4. stairs   8. python   12. lucky

---

30.   1. toast   5. flat   9. midway

            2. today   6. flesh   10. mighty

            3. tomato   7. floor   11. minute

            4. toxin   8. flute   12. mite

---

32.   1. long

            2. no sound (or similar answer)

            3. Answers vary.

Answer Key (pages 33-38)

Page:

33.
1. met

2. sit

3. Should contain a macron: bē, tīme, hōse

4. **b)** It makes a long sound.

5. macron

35.

1. bāby   3. todāy   5. ōpen   6. ēnough

7. game   9. take   10. say

13. They are marked with a macron.

14. They are not marked.

36.
1. <u>**3**</u>

2. <u>**2**</u>

3. <u>**2**</u>

4. <u>**2**</u>

37.
1. exit

2. wasp

3. laden

4. love

38.
1. masthead   3. bagel

2. mumble

Answer Key (pages 39-43)

Page:

39.   1. They have macrons over them.

2. ā ē ī ō

3. a e i o

4. The long vowels have macrons and the short vowels have no markings.

5. parentheses.

6. separated.

---

40.   maple

---

42.   Answers vary.

---

43.   1. pok´ ət

2. nib´ əl

3. blub´ ər

4. chik´ ən

5. shiv´ ər

6. rit´ ər

7. tem´ pər

8. pə lēs´ mən

Answer Key (pages 44-51)

Page:

44.
1.	**3**	**for´**	
2.	**3**	**owt´**	
3.	**2**	**lan´**	
4.	**4**	**spesh´**	
5.	**3**	**man´**	
6.	**3**	**nēr´**	
7.	**5**	**kred´**	
8.	**4**	**lā´**	
9.	**2**	**plāt´**	
10.	**2**	**twen´**	

49.
1. b) languor
2. c) three
3. b) lignite

51.
1. verb
2. noun
3. adjective
4. verb
5. verb
6. Answers vary.
7. Answers vary.

Answer Key (pages 53-56)

Page:

53.   1. c

            2. b

            3. a

---

55.   1. line

            2. popcorn

            3. 3

            4. 4

            5. 5

            6. iceberg

            7. idea

            8. impeach

            9. impede

---

56.   10. lame

            11. lament

            12. lamp

            13. land

            14. orangutan

            15. 4

            16. 2

            17. fortissimo

www.ingramcontent.com/pod-product-compliance
Lightning Source LLC
Chambersburg PA
CBHW081545040426
42448CB00015B/3230